D0898651

The LeBaron Russell Briggs Prize
Honors Essays in English · 1965

HAWTHORNE'S CONCEPTION
OF THE CREATIVE PROCESS

HAWTHORNE'S CONCEPTION OF THE CREATIVE PROCESS

Richard J. Jacobson

HARVARD UNIVERSITY PRESS
Cambridge, Massachusetts

To David Perkins

CONTENTS

HAWTHORNE'S CONCEPTION
OF THE CREATIVE PROCESS

HAWTHORNE'S CONCEPTION
OF THE CREATIVE PROCESS

This study aims at an examination of the processes of mind that Hawthorne viewed as underlying creativity. A presentation of the matrix of theory that influenced Hawthorne and served as a vehicle for the expression of his attitudes will be followed by an attempt to define his conception of the creative process. His writings on the subject are loose, but suggestive. It was his own romantic tendency to value an art that "suggests far more than it shows." [1] Viewed in this light, Hawthorne's comments on the creative process are neither hard and fast dicta nor deliberately obscure and elusive circumventions. They are rooted deeply in an understanding of himself and the tradition, both continental and American, that informs his own writing.

Hawthorne's extensive reading covered contemporary American Transcendentalists, the English Romantics, the Augustans, and included a thorough knowledge of Spenser and Milton.[2] A remark to Sophia Peabody possibly reveals the extent to which Transcendentalist idealism figured in his thinking: "How much mud and mire, how many pools of unclean water, how many slippery footsteps, and perchance heavy tumbles, might be avoided, if we could tread but six inches above the crust of this world." [3] Hawthorne's concern with "suggestiveness," and with "multëity in unity," is rooted in romantic theories of art. His stylistic tendencies demonstrate a thorough knowledge of Johnson and other writers of the eighteenth century. It is Spenser who most directly influenced his allegorical techniques and use of character "types." And, finally, Hawthorne's evaluation of the American experience as a fall from innocence finds, among several sources, a conceptual model in *Paradise Lost*.[4]

On the basis of his reading alone it is difficult to consider Hawthorne as an isolated genius, separated from all outside influences. The conflicts that surround his views on creativity can best be seen as evolving from the divergent strains in his intellectual background. What is individual and isolated in Hawthorne is the refraction of these intellectual cross-currents through the medium of his personality.

Several conflicts that mark the transition from classic to romantic are embodied in Hawthorne's conception of the creative process, but particularly the "organic-mechanical antithesis," [5] and the changing metaphors of mind from the mirror to the lamp, Aeolian harp, or fountain.[6] Familiar with the writings of Carlyle,[7] Hawthorne was most certainly exposed to the "organic-mechanical antithesis" in "Signs of the Times," or in *Sartor Resartus*. The importance of Carlyle's influence in America is reflected in a notice that appeared in *The Dial* of July 1841: "Although the name of Thomas Carlyle is rarely mentioned in the critical journals of this country, there is no living writer who is more sure of immediate attention from a large circle of readers or who exercises a greater influence than he in these United States."[8] It was Carlyle's hope that the organic and the mechanical could exist in a balance; he feared unchecked self-expression leading to chaos as much as he did the crushing of the individual by the machine.

In "Old Ticonderoga" Hawthorne describes his visit to the fort with a West Point lieutenant who served as his guide. Of the young man's lectures he writes: "His description of Ticonderoga would be as accurate as a geometrical theorem, and as barren of the poetry that has clustered round its decay."[9] The mechanical is not the realm of art, and in its place Hawthorne substitutes the organic metaphor. In the preface to the *Twice-Told Tales* he likens his work to "flowers which blossomed in too retired a shade."[10] The tales and essays in *Mosses from an Old Manse* "blossomed out like flowers in the calm summer" of his "heart and mind."[11] "The ripened autumnal fruit" is the harvest of *The Snow-Image*. Hawthorne's metaphor is close to Carlyle's appeal to organic nature at the end of "The Everlasting Yea," but on a much lower key.

Through Coleridge, Hawthorne was exposed directly to the concept of an organic art. Coleridge's remark that the imagination is "a repetition in the finite mind of the eternal act of creation" finds a parallel in Hawthorne's comment on the "painful" detail of a painting by Millais: "It is not well to be so perfect in the inanimate, unless the artist can likewise make man and woman as lifelike — and to as great a depth too — as the Creator does." [12] Coleridge says of Shakespeare that he worked by "evolving the germ within." Hawthorne's preference for the sketch to the final work of art reflects his fear that the artist will cover the "celestial germ" with layers of his own personality, and prevent the flowering of the "innermost germ" [13] into a full organic whole. The Cathedral of Siena impressed Hawthorne because it combined "a majesty and a minuteness, neither interfering with the other, each assisting the other." It seemed to him a "solemn whole," a fusion of "minute particulars." [14] Here he shares the notion of Coleridge that art is a unification emerging through "multëity" — a fusion "to force many into one." [15] Hawthorne writes of the creator of the Laocoön: "It was a most powerful mind, and one capable of reducing a complex idea to unity, that imagined this group." [16] What counts then in art is not merely diversity but the intensity of the fusion to which minute particulars are subjected. Like Coleridge, he conceives of art as a means and not an end — in W. J. Bate's terms, "a way of rendering truth realizable to the total mind, through the medium of humanly persuasive symbols." [17] Coleridge's notion of beauty as a "calling on the soul" is reflected in Hawthorne's reaction to the fresco of Christ bound to a pillar by Sodoma: "This hallowed work of genius shows what pictorial art, devoutly exercised, might effect in behalf of religious truth; involving, as it does, deeper mysteries of revelation, and bringing them closer to man's heart, and making him tenderer to be impressed by them, than the most eloquent words of preacher or prophet." [18]

For Hawthorne the most explicit demonstration of "reducing a complex idea to unity" is in the Gothic style of architecture. The Cathedral of Lichfield seems to him a perfect example of Gothic sublimity: "Then there are such strange, delightful recesses in the great figure of the Cathedral; it is so difficult to melt it all into one idea and comprehend it in that way; and yet it is all so consonant in its intricacy — it seems to me a Gothic Cathedral may be the greatest work man has yet achieved — a great stone poem." [19] As Maurice Charney points out, Hawthorne was most powerfully impressed by the "multitudinousness" of the Gothic style — its ability to fashion a wealth of detail into a rich organic whole.[20]

The impact of the Gothic style rests also in its capacity to elicit a broad response through a "double perspective" — "surely these medieval works have an advantage over the classic; they combine the telescope and the microscope." [21] Here Hawthorne's appeal is on behalf of a more expressive art in which multiple perspectives contribute to a dynamic unfolding of form through matter. Gothic springs from "the dim, awful, mysterious, grotesque, intricate nature of man," [22] and is "moistened with human life-blood." [23] It is the product of human feelings and emotions and strives beyond "the classic coldness which is as repellent as the touch of marble." [24]

Hawthorne's rebellion against classicism, however, is neither clear-cut nor thoroughgoing. His evaluation of Gothic, and art in general, is rooted in the greatest of classical premises (a premise that ultimately underlies all serious evaluations of art) — the conviction that art is formative.[25] In a letter to Sophia Peabody he states that beauty is love, "and therefore includes both truth and good." Furthermore, "only those who love can feel the significance and force of this."[26] The awareness that great art can guide and form man's responses infiltrates Hawthorne's critical judgments. Of a fresco in Santa Maria degl'Angeli he writes: "The nail-marks in the hands and feet of Jesus, ineffaceable, even after he had passed into bliss and glory, touched my heart with a sense of his love for us. I think this really a great picture."[27] The imagination of the beholder, directed outwards, is able to identify with what it perceives. Art, then, in its highest sense, can be directly formative. Hence the focus of the imagination must always be on beauty and truth; otherwise one becomes, as Hawthorne frequently warns, an idle observer who gives up his own identity without the reward of truth. As Coleridge remarks, "The heart should have fed upon the truth, as insects on a leaf, till it be tinged with the colour, and show its food in every minutest fibre."

In addition to the powerful influence of Coleridge,[28] Ruskin finds his way into Hawthorne's critical judgments. Una Hawthorne wrote to Elizabeth Peabody, December 31, 1856: "Papa brought a book from the Library called 'The Modern Painters,' by Ruskin."[29] It is not certain that Hawthorne read *The Stones of Venice*, but his appreciation of the "multitudinousness" of the Gothic style is similar to Ruskin's criteria of "changefulness" and "redundance." For Ruskin these are the "moral elements of Gothic," and similarly, for Hawthorne, multiplicity is transformed from an aesthetic to a moral criterion. He was able to enjoy classical architecture, but felt that it never moved his heart as deeply as the Gothic. Because art is viewed as formative, the classical style is deprecated on moral grounds: "I always see great beauty and lightsomeness in these classic and Grecian edifices, though they seem cold and intellectual, and not to have had their mortar moistened with human life-blood, nor to have the mystery of human life in them, as Gothic structures do." [30] Gothic is a higher art because it appeals to a broader base of human feeling; it has the quality of "love" that Hawthorne proposes as a definition of beauty.

Concerning his attempt to make classical myths "very capital reading for children" in *A Wonder-Book*, Hawthorne wrote in a letter to Fields: "I shall aim at substituting a tone in some degree Gothic or romantic, or any such tone as may best please myself, instead of the classic." [31] In the preface Hawthorne states that the myths have "perhaps assumed a Gothic or romantic guise." Furthermore, the classic is hard and clear in its outlines, and something into which Gothic will breathe life and feeling. The inter-chapters of *A Wonder-Book* carry on the debate between classic and romantic. The

8

narrator, young Eustace, defends Gothic against the arguments of Mr. Pringle. To a degree, the debate reflects Hawthorne's internal conflict over literary theory. Mr. Pringle tells Eustace: "Your imagination is altogether Gothic, and will inevitably Gothicize everything that you touch. The effect is like bedaubing a marble statue with paint. This giant, now! How can you have ventured to thrust his huge, disproportioned mass among the seemly outlines of Grecian fable, the tendency of which is to reduce even the extravagant within limits, by its pervading elegance?" To this defense of the classic on the basis of proportion and clarity of outline Eustace answers: "The moment you put any warmth of heart, any passion or affection, any human or divine morality, into a classic mould, you make it quite another thing from what it was before. My own opinion is, that the Greeks, by taking possession of these legends . . . and putting them into shapes of indestructible beauty, indeed, but cold and heartless, have done all subsequent ages an incalculable injury." [32] Although Eustace comes out on top, the conflict does not seem totally resolved in Hawthorne's mind.

The classic-romantic antithesis is at the root of Hawthorne's distinction between the novel and the romance.[33] The novel aims "at a very minute fidelity, not merely to the possible, but to the probable and ordinary course of man's experience." The novel is drawn on classical lines, with a clarity and sharpness of form. The romance, on the other hand, claims a "certain latitude, both as to its fashion and material," but remains faithful to the "truth of the human heart." In its moonlit world suggestiveness is substituted for clarity of outline, and the author "may so manage his atmospherical medium as to bring out or mellow the lights and deepen and enrich the shadows of the picture." As long as a romancer remains true to the human heart "he has a right to present that truth under circumstances" which are of his "own choosing or creation." [34] The romance is an outgrowth of expressive theories of art in which the "internal is made external." [35] Hawthorne's attempt to justify the choice of Brook Farm as a setting for *The Blithedale Romance* — "merely to establish a theatre, a little removed from the highway of ordinary travel, where the creatures of his brain may play their phantasmagorical antics, without exposing them to too close a comparison with the actual events of real lives" — becomes an appeal for an expressive theory of art over and above the mimetic.[36]

Hawthorne's kinship with romantic critical theory is demonstrated throughout his writings. But there are many classical elements in his thought all too frequently ignored.[37] At the other extreme are critics like Henry

Kariel who try to make a case for a thoroughgoing classicism, but their view does not do justice to Hawthorne's broad and eclectic understanding of art.[38] Hawthorne's conception of the creative process represents, in fact, a fusion of classic and romantic attitudes. In Hawthorne they are not incompatible and their fusion gives his views originality and fullness.

Hawthorne's regard for the eighteenth century is higher, on the whole, than for any other age in English literature.[39] For an American in his century he had an unusually sound appreciation of the English Augustans. After a walk among the streets of London he wrote: "I think what interests me most here is the London of the writers of the Queen Anne age — whatever Pope, the Spectator, De Foe, and down as late as Johnson and Goldsmith have mentioned." He called Pope's description of the kitchen at Stanton Harcourt "one of the most admirable pieces of description in the language." He traveled to Lichfield partly to see the beautiful cathedral and partly "because it was the birthplace of Dr. Johnson," and to Uttoxeter ("one of the few purely sentimental pilgrimages that I ever undertook") to visit the scene of Dr. Johnson's penance. At a time when Dr. Johnson was out of fashion he praised "London" and "The Vanity of Human Wishes" for "stern and masculine" qualities, and commended

Dr. Johnson's morality as "wholesome food even now."[40] It is not strange then that Hawthorne's treatment of the imagination as a mirror owes a debt to English neoclassicism.

Millicent Bell, in her analysis of Hawthorne's classical tendencies, attempts to apply Morse Peckham's concept of "negative romanticism" — "the expression of the feelings and ideas of a man who has left the static mechanism of the eighteenth-century world behind, but has not yet arrived at the transcendentalist reintegration."[41] This approach — wrongheaded because it desperately struggles to find a neat category into which Hawthorne can be placed — proceeds on the mistaken assumptions that neoclassical theory necessarily upholds a "static mechanism," and that "pure romanticism" is characterized by a "transcendentalist reintegration." The neoclassicism to which Hawthorne was exposed, primarily through Burke and Johnson, sees the world organically, with a sense of its dynamic process, and certainly Coleridge's romanticism does not "shrink from reality"[42] to hover, as the Transcendentalists, above the crust of the earth. The crucial point to be made here is that Hawthorne's adoption of neoclassical and romantic theory is focused on the attempt to validate his own imaginative insights; and his theorizing on art moves inexorably toward this end.

Hawthorne is always faithful to the idea that "this world is not the place to pour out the soul without reserve." [43] He would partially agree with Emerson that "words cannot cover the dimensions of what is in truth," that they "break, chop, and impoverish it." [44] But according to Hawthorne this would apply more directly to a misuse of language. Furthermore, any artificial construct of the mind, such as Hollingsworth's philanthropy in *The Blithedale Romance*, distorts and deforms life. Hawthorne always fears this distortion, and, by dwelling on it, seems to apply his own corrective. Describing the valley of Perugia he writes: "No language nor any art of the pencil can give an idea of the scene. When God expressed himself in the landscape to mankind, He did not intend that it should be translated into any tongue save his own immediate one." [45] Of his attempt to describe "autumnal brilliancies" he says: "I have tried a thousand times, and always without the slightest self-satisfaction." [46] This kind of frustration occurs repeatedly throughout his notebooks, and suggests that Hawthorne's view of art is rooted deeply in the awareness of man's limitations. Pure Transcendentalism, in denying any limits, does not really make the job of creation any easier. Margaret Fuller, suggests Hawthorne, had forgotten who created her, and "took credit to herself for having been her own Redeemer

. . . But she was not working on inanimate substance, like marble or clay; there was something within her that she could not possibly come at, to re-create it and refine it; and, by and by, this rude old potency bestirred itself, and undid all her labor in the twinkling of an eye." [47] Similarly, in "The Birthmark," Aylmer is unable to transcend the limits of ordinary humanity through the powers of his art. And Rappaccini's garden is such that "the production was no longer of God's making, but the monstrous offspring of man's depraved fancy, glowing with only an evil mockery of beauty." [48]

The egotism that refuses to accept any limitations is condemned on aesthetic as well as moral grounds. Hawthorne's preference is for an art that deals with "human nature in the mass," and not merely "human character in its individual developments." [49] One is reminded of Johnson's dictum that "nothing can please many, and please long, but just representations of general nature." The artist's purpose is to remain faithful to his materials, to the life that he seeks to portray. It is with this in mind that Hawthorne writes: "So far as I am a man of really individual attributes I veil my face; nor am I, nor have I ever been, one of those supremely hospitable people who serve up their own hearts, delicately fried, with brain sauce, as a tidbit for their beloved public." [50] With a measure of modesty as well as frustration Hawthorne reflects: "How narrow — how shallow and scanty too — is the stream of thought that has been flowing from my pen, compared with the broad tide of dim emotions, ideas, and associations which swell around me." [51]

2

The state of mind that produces creative insight is seen by Hawthorne as analogous to the "singular moment . . . when you have hardly begun to recollect yourself, after starting from midnight slumber." To put it another way: "You find yourself, for a single instant, wide awake in that realm of illusions, whither sleep has been the passport." In an hour like this the mind has a "passive sensibility, but no active strength," and "the imagination is a mirror, imparting vividness to all ideas, without the power of selecting or controlling them." A series of fresh impressions, images from the "dark receptacles" that are "in the depths of every heart," arise to "haunt" the mind.[52] Coleridge, in his retrospective preface to "Kubla Khan," describes a similar experience, adding, of course, that he composed the poem in a profound sleep, "if that indeed can be called composition in which all the images rose up before [me] as things, with a parallel production

15

of the correspondent expressions, without any sensation or consciousness of effort." [53] Hazlitt, too, speaks of "a state between sleeping and waking," where we have "indistinct but glorious glimpses of strange shapes." [54] Hawthorne insists that the mind has no active strength during moments of passive sensibility, and that it is fully receptive to the images arising from the depths of the heart. Unlike Emerson, he refuses to make the creative process an act of will.

The sensation of waking at midnight, explored in "The Haunted Mind," is typical of the psychological state most conducive to creativity. Images, "in which Passion and Feeling assume bodily shape," [55] become accessible to the artist. As in Spenser's processions of allegorical figures, Sorrow, Hope, Disappointment, Fatality, and Shame rise in "a funeral train" before Hawthorne's eyes. The description of the creative process in Poe's *Marginalia* is remarkably similar: images "arise in the soul . . . only at its epochs of most intense tranquility, and at those mere points of time where the confines of the waking world blend with those of the world of dreams." [56] For Hawthorne these images are not at all part of a conscious thought process. It is in this light that one should view his comment that a stream of thought is shallow and small "compared with the broad tide of dim emotions, ideas, associations, which were flowing through the haunted regions of imagination." [57]

The source of the images in the "depths of the heart" is the sense impressions that rise out of experience. Hawthorne feels that man is open to experience in two ways: through what he is able to learn by observing nature, man, society and its dominant values, essentially what he rationally acquires, and through feelings and conflicts that are shared by all men. The latter, which Jung calls the "collective unconscious," Hawthorne designates as that sense in man "which gives the human spirit so deep an insight into its fellows and melts all humanity into one cordial heart of hearts." [58]

Experience through observation is a possession of the scientist. Rappaccini's garden springs from the knowledge that he uncovers through scientific investigation. His look, "as deep as Nature itself," reflects a preternatural knowledge of life, but he is without "Nature's warmth of love." His garden is an "adultery of various vegetable species," and glows "with only an evil mockery of beauty." [59] In other words, Rappaccini draws on only one source of experience, and quite forgets the bond of feelings and emotions that unites all men. Similarly, Miles Coverdale is a mere observer, isolated in his leafy hermitage. He suspects that his attempt to learn the secret of people "hidden even from themselves" reflects a "vulgar curiosity." But Coverdale has a rudimentary awareness of another level of experience that permits art to proceed "by generous sympathies, by delicate intuitions, by taking note of things too slight for record, and by bringing my human spirit into manifold accordance with the companions whom God assigned me." [60]

As a general corrective to passionless inquiry, Hawthorne would advocate "tenderness of sentiment," [61] an awareness of feelings that are the communal experience of all men. What man learns through rational inquiry becomes useful in art only if it is made part of the larger scheme of shared, universal experience. It is Hawthorne's tendency in art, as in life, to trust intuition rather than analytical reason. He suggests that if the multitude forms its judgments "on the intuitions of its great and warm heart, the conclusions thus attained are often so profound and so unerring, as to possess the character of truths supernaturally revealed."[62] The "Unpardonable Sin," for Hawthorne, consists in a "want of love and reverence for the Human Soul" which is typified by the man who pries into the depths of the heart with "a cold philosophical curiosity." The result, fatal in art, as well as in relationships among men, is a "separation of the intellect from the heart." [63]

Experience from observation and feelings, then, is reconstructed in the mind in images. The "opaque substance of today" [64] (a part of life open to rational analysis), and the "depths of our common nature" [65] are both the primary sources of these images. They, in turn, are stored by what Hawthorne designates as the fancy. But these "glittering icicles of fancy" [66] are merely cold outlines, without the warmth of life. It is the task of the artist to convert them from a "truth . . . only in the fancy" to a "substance in the mind and heart." [67] The fancy, in its cold "tendency to abstraction," [68] is separated from the characteristically living qualities of nature.[69] (For Hawthorne, an abstraction would have the special meaning of an image that is not warmed in the heart.) The art of pure fancy, of "snow-images," is dominated by the wish to escape the flux and pain of life. It takes refuge in permanent and durable abstractions from what T. E. Hulme calls "the varied confusion and arbitrariness of existence."

Out of this feeling of isolation and separation from life "we have allegory, not always so warmly dressed in its habiliments of flesh and blood as to be taken into the reader's mind without a shiver." [70] Similarly,

Drowne's carvings, except for one inspired work of genius, are lacking in "the one touch . . . that would be truly valuable," and which would make the "figure of General Wolfe, for instance, a breathing and intelligent human creature." [71] The sonnet, "To the Snow on Mount Washington," written by the poet in "Sketches from Memory," "was elegant and full of fancy." Thus the lines were "too remote from familiar sentiment, and cold as their subject, resembling those curious specimens of crystallized vapor which I observed next day on the mountain top." [72] Of the detailed accuracy in William Page's portrait of Browning, Hawthorne remarks that the "accumulation of minute truths did not, after all, amount to the true whole." [73] Nor does Thomas Crawford's statue of Washington impress Hawthorne as "having grown out of any genuine idea in the artist's mind, but being merely an ingenious contrivance enough." [74] The artist "endowed with a beautiful fancy" is rejected in favor of one who "has studied Nature with such tender love that she takes him to her intimacy, enabling him to reproduce her in landscapes that seem the reality of a better earth, and yet are but the truth of the very scenes around us." In contrast to the "very dextrous and capable" artists of fancy — "smart practical men" who had probably won credit for high skill "by the nice carving of button-holes, shoe-ties, coat-seams, shirt bosoms, and other such graceful peculiarities of modern costume" — Hawthorne extols Praxiteles, whose Faun harkens back to "a period when man's affinity with nature was more strict, and his fellowship with every living thing more intimate and dear." [75] The ideal of fellowship is present in true art, and stands behind Hawthorne's comment on his tales that they were attempts, "and very imperfectly successful ones, to open an intercourse with the world." [76]

It is possible that Coleridge's distinction between fancy and imagination in the *Biographia Literaria* influenced Hawthorne's method of conceptualizing the antithesis. (Hawthorne borrowed this work from the Salem Athenaeum on October 29, 1836, and returned it on December 10.)[77] Even if his ideas are not taken directly from Coleridge, it is still suggestive to focus on certain similarities. The imagination, for Coleridge, is essentially vital, "even as all objects (as objects) are essentially fixed and dead," but the fancy, on the contrary, "has no other counters to play with, but fixities and definites. The fancy is indeed no other than a mode of memory emancipated from the order of time and space." Furthermore, "the fancy must receive all its materials ready made from the law of association." [78] Hawthorne, too, views the fancy as a mode of memory, a storehouse of sense impressions which derive from experience. Like Coleridge, he conceives of the fancy as having the power to form combinations and patterns of association among various images. The "association of ideas," which Hawthorne accepts as a major function of the fancy, goes back, as a concept, to English empirical psychology, and more specifically, to David Hartley, with whose writings Hawthorne was familiar. Roughly, the "association of ideas" suggests, among other things, that, given a certain order of steps in a thought process, or a certain order of images, the intervening steps may "lapse," and the sight or thought of the first will lead immediately to the last, giving the impression of a sudden intuition.[79] With perhaps this in mind, Hawthorne would claim that an "artist of fancy" possesses technical facility, and even an apparently profound intuitive sense, but that his works, on closer inspection, are without the warmth of imagination and depth of sympathy that signify true greatness in art. Hawthorne's preference for an art of generous sympathies to an art of fancy underlies his judgment of Saint Paul's Cathedral: "It is a grand edifice, and I liked it quite as much as on my first view of it; although a sense of coldness and nakedness is felt, when we compare it with Gothic churches; — it is more an external affair than the Gothic churches are, and is not so made out of the dim, awful, mysterious, grotesque, intricate nature of man." [80]

In the best art, according to Hawthorne — an art that establishes multiple points of contact with feelings and experiences common to all men — "a heart and sensibilities of human tenderness" are communicated to the "forms which fancy summons up." They are converted "from snow-images into men and women." [81] When an image infiltrates into the heart, and is tinged by the color of feelings, it becomes a persuasive and moving symbol. Thus the creations of the fancy become full-fledged symbols only when they are bathed in the "surging stream of human sympathies," in the "mighty river of life, massive in its tide, and black with mystery." [82] A central concern of Hawthorne is to transmute what is personal and idiosyncratic into symbols that share in "our common nature." Or, as he states the idea in *The Marble Faun*, "the warm and pure suggestions of a woman's heart" give Miriam "a force and variety of imaginative sympathies" that enable her "to fill her life richly with the bliss and suffering of womanhood, however barren it might individually be." [83]

Behind Hawthorne's thought that every human endeavor must be guided by "heart-knowledge" is the great value he places on the sympathetic powers of the mind. Images that are given life and warmth become generally applicable to the whole range of human experience because the heart of every individual, to some extent, participates in the "cordial heart of hearts" that furnishes a tie among men. When the artist is able to identify with what is universal in himself, his creations bear the stamp of love for the life around him. Thus Hawthorne praises Shelley's more mature poems because "the author has learned to dip his pen oftener into his heart, and has thereby avoided the faults in to which a too exclusive use of fancy and intellect are wont to betray him." [84] The sympathy behind a work of art also underlies the reaction of a person who beholds it. The reader of Shelley's best poetry, for example, takes the meaning into his heart, and is conscious of "a heart warmth responsive" to his own. With a similar idea in his mind, Hawthorne says of Byron that "his passions having burned out, the extinction of their vivid and riotous flame has deprived him of the illumination by which he not merely wrote, but was enabled to feel and comprehend what he had written." [85]

The art of Drowne the woodcarver generally suffers from a lack of sympathy and love, the basic ingredients of inspiration. Although he has a powerful fancy, and "no inconsiderable skill of hand, nor a deficiency of any attribute" to render his statues "really works of art," he fails in "that deep quality, be it of soul or intellect, which bestows life upon the lifeless and warmth upon the cold." But in the creation of the Oaken Lady, his one masterpiece, Drowne works with his "whole strength, and soul, and faith," inspired by a "wellspring of inward wisdom." As the artist Copley recognizes, the statue is a product of "human love which, in a spiritual sense . . . was the secret of the life that had been breathed into this block of wood." In a fleeting moment of inspired creativity Drowne is possessed with a genius "kindled by love," which renders him a great artist for that one occasion, but afterwards leaves him again "the mechanical carver in wood, without the power even of appreciating the work that his own hands had wrought." Hawthorne speculates, and this is crucial to his conception of the creative process, "that the very highest state to which a human spirit can attain, in its loftiest aspirations, is its truest and most natural state, and that Drowne was more consistent with himself when he wrought the admirable figure of the mysterious lady, than when he perpetrated a whole progeny of blockheads." [86] The artist is perhaps most individual, and most "himself," when he is transported through love to a sympathetic identification with the objects of his art. Hawthorne seems to imply, in a typically romantic way, that in the apex of creative intensity the artist goes beyond his superficial layers of personality, inspired by love and sympathy, to reach something more basic in himself and in the experience he seeks to describe. The resulting work of art embodies "beauty" in a way that has the highest meaning for Hawthorne: "it is love, and therefore includes both truth and good." [87]

The danger for the artist is that he might become "insulated from the common business of life" and, as a result, experience "a sensation of moral cold that makes the spirit shiver as if it had reached the frozen solitudes around the pole." Owen Warland is Hawthorne's archetypal artist of the fancy, one who is separated from human sympathies. In his childhood Owen "had been remarkable for a delicate ingenuity" which sometimes seemed "to aim at the hidden mysteries of mechanism." He had a "love of the beautiful . . . completely refined from all utilitarian coarseness." The culmination of his artistic maturity, the fruit of a lonely life in which he divorces himself from the satisfactions of a wife and family, is an object of "glory . . . splendor . . . delicate gorgeousness" — a mechanical butterfly. There is a strong sense of irony that stands behind Hawthorne's choice of a mechanical butterfly to symbolize Owen's highest achievement. It is not merely useless (Hawthorne would never condemn a work of art on this ground), but it does not reflect the experiences of joy and suffering that comprise the fabric of human life. The butterfly is a delicate, evanescent creation of a man who has withdrawn from the world. So when Owen watches the destruction of his "masterpiece" in the hands of the little child, he is unable to feel even the slightest trace of sorrow. "He had caught a far other butterfly than this. When the artist rose high enough to achieve the beautiful, the symbol by which he made it perceptible to mortal senses became of little value in his eyes while his spirit possessed itself in the enjoyment of the reality." [88] Owen is so lost in a "squeamish love of the beautiful" [89] that he is beyond even the ordinary human reaction of grief. It is precisely because he forsakes the whole realm of human sympathies that his art is without the warmth of feeling and generosity of love essential to any durable creation. Art comes to Owen, and Walter Pater's words express this admirably, professing frankly to give nothing but the highest quality to his moments as they pass, and simply for those moments' sake. The single-minded quest for intense aesthetic experience, which loses all reference to life and common nature, is condemned by Hawthorne as the most insidious form of egotism because it leaves the man it possesses with the illusion that he has dedicated his life to a higher cause.

When the creative process is not cut off at the fancy, and images are transformed into symbols, the art that results appeals directly to a broad range of human feelings and values. It is an art that rises above Owen Warland's aestheticism to furnish an evaluation of man's collective experience within the specific framework of the artist's symbols.

On the most basic level Hawthorne believes that a symbol is a combination of images, under the law of association of ideas, evolving into a dynamic representation of general experience. To put it another way, a fancy is more nearly an idiosyncratic representation of individual experience; whereas a symbol stands for the deeper meaning of man's encounter with the world. Owen Warland's mechanical butterfly is a fancy; the scarlet letter is a symbol.

Each word, for Hawthorne, is potentially a symbol because it partakes of a language that men employ communally, and is the smallest unit of man's shared experience. As Hawthorne remarks: "Words — so innocent and powerless as they are, as standing in a dictionary, how potent for good and evil they become, in the hands of one who knows how to use them." [90] He would agree with Wordsworth's comment that language improperly used is "unremittingly and noiselessly at work, to subvert, to lay waste, to vitiate, and to dissolve." [91] But a more striking resemblance in this matter of symbolism is between Hawthorne and Coleridge.[92] Coleridge asserts in his comment on Horne Tooke's *Epea Pteroenta*, "winged words: or language, not only the vehicle of thought but the wheels . . . The wheels of the intellect I admit them to be, but such as Ezekiel beheld in the *visions of God* as he sate among the captives by the river of Chebar. *Whithersoever the Spirit was to go, the wheels went, and thither was their Spirit to go; for the Spirit of the living creature was in the wheels also.*" [93] Here Coleridge suggests that a word is a symbol. The symbol, in the sense that Coleridge attaches to the term, reconciles opposites such as sensation and thought, matter and spirit, the individual and the universal.[94] In the *Statesman's Manual* Coleridge amplifies the thought in stating that the imagination "gives birth to a system of symbols, harmonious in themselves and consubstantial with the truths of which they are the conductors. These are the *wheels* which Ezekiel beheld, when the hand of the Lord was upon him." [95] Words (and Hawthorne supports this view) are not merely the medium of communication. They are themselves the live power of thought and, as such, are essential to deep feeling and understanding. But Hawthorne goes beyond Coleridge in the recognition that thought can be nonverbal, in the form of images, and hence possess a greater nuance of meaning.

The symbolic imagination fuses "the real world and fairyland, where the Actual and the Imaginary may meet, and each imbue itself with the nature of the other." [96] It serves as a mediator between the individual life and the community of men. Thus the artist has "a religious obligation" [97] to his materials; it is his responsibility to open an intercourse between his own "inner drama" and the external world,[98] and, analogously, to reconcile each man to the "dark necessity" of life.[99] As Auden was to remark a century later, the use of language becomes a theological question.[100]

The power of a symbol to fuse personal fancy and the experiences of the "collective unconscious" is the subject of a strange and elusive comment in one of Hawthorne's notebooks: "To make literal pictures of figurative expressions; — for instance, he burst into tears — a man suddenly turned into a shower of briny drops. An explosion of laughter — a man blowing up, and his fragments flying about on all sides. He cast his eyes upon the ground — a man standing eyeless, with his eyes on the ground, staring up at him in wonderment." [101] In this bizarre thought Hawthorne is struggling to convey the feeling that words have a powerful reality and life for the artist. The symbolic language of art fuses the literal and the figurative, the actual and the imaginary, and is sacred because it is part of life itself. Words, as symbols, have an important role in channeling feelings, and art, at its best, can "disclose treasures in some unexpected cave of truth," [102] "bringing them closer to man's heart, and making him tenderer to be impressed by them."[103] In its broadest meaning for Hawthorne, a symbol is an imitation of our common nature, of the dynamic and creative force of life, in terms appropriate to the personal experience of the artist. As such, it is able to present individual experience, in its multiplicity and ambiguity of meaning, as universal experience. Thus the vision of the artist penetrates to the essence of life. As Hawthorne says: "What is called poetic insight is the gift of discerning, in this sphere of strangely mingled elements, the beauty and the majesty which are compelled to assume a garb so sordid." [104]

In Hawthorne's conception of the creative process the imagination serves to mirror the symbols of the heart and to deepen man's awareness by infiltrating these symbols into the conscious mind.

The mirror is Hawthorne's most persistent metaphor of imagination. In praise of Shakespeare, Johnson wrote that "his drama is the mirrour of life." Hawthorne goes further in a special direction — away from realism — in saying that whatever is "unsightly in reality, assumes ideal beauty in the reflection." [105] Furthermore, a mirror "is always a kind of window or doorway into the spiritual world." [106] Of his trip down the Assabeth River with Ellery Channing, Hawthorne writes: "The slumbering river has a dream picture in its bosom. Which, after all, was the most real — the picture, or the original? — the objects palpable to our grosser senses, or their apotheosis in the stream beneath? Surely the disembodied images stand in closer relation to the soul." [107] Many years later at Stratford he remarked that the Avon may have held Shakespeare's "gorgeous visions . . . in its bosom." [108] The mirror is seen as reflecting the essence or form of reality. And it may also penetrate beneath sordid moral sham as in "Feathertop." There the mirror is "one of the truest plates in the world and incapable of flattery." When Feathertop regards himself in the full-length looking glass he sees not "the glittering mockery of his outside show, but a picture of the sordid patchwork of his real composition." [109] By penetrating deeply into life, and disengaging actuality from appearance,[110] the mirror, like the imagination, serves a moral function. It can picture the ideal — not the Transcendentalist ideal treading "six inches above the crust of this world" — but one that expresses, in Butcher's terms, "a purified form of reality disengaged from accident, and freed from conditions which thwart its development." [111]

To regard oneself in a mirror, as Hawthorne does in "Monsieur du Miroir," is a sobering experience: "There is something fearful in bearing such a relation to a creature so imperfectly known, and in the idea that, to a certain extent, all which concerns myself will be reflected in its consequences upon him." Reflecting on the power of the mirror image to follow him, Hawthorne writes: "I will compare the attempt to escape him to the hopeless race that men sometimes run with memory, or their own hearts, or their moral selves, which, though burdened with cares enough to crush an elephant, will never be one step behind." [112] Similarly, in *The Scarlet Letter*, in the chapter called "The Interior of a Heart," Dimmesdale views his own face in a mirror "by the most powerful light which he could throw upon it," and thus "typified the constant introspection wherewith he tortured, but could not purify himself." When Chillingworth realizes that he has been transformed into a fiend through his persecution of Dimmesdale, he lifts his hands with a look of horror, "as if he had beheld some frightful shape, which he could not recognize, usurping the place of his own image in a glass. It was one of those moments

— which sometimes occur only at the interval of years — when a man's moral aspect is faithfully revealed to his mind's eye." [113] The "mind's eye," or the imagination, is the instrument of moral insight. By divesting life from appearances it is able to see things as they are, to see morally. This moral vision transcends temporal limitations to achieve a perception of unchanging forms. But the extent to which imaginings are "valid" depends upon the individual. In *The House of the Seven Gables*, when all the characters have left for better surroundings, Maule's Well, "though left in solitude, was throwing up a succession of kaleidoscopic pictures, in which a *gifted eye* might have seen foreshadowed the coming fortunes." [114]

It is necessary to point out, as does F. O. Matthiessen, that when Hawthorne speaks of the imagination as a mirror he is not in complete agreement with classical or neoclassical theory. The ultimate function of the imagination, according to Hawthorne, is not to reflect external reality, but to reflect the creations of one's own heart, "imparting vividness to all ideas, without the power of selecting or controlling them." [115] But at other times he speaks of the imagination as a lamp, "a light which seemed to hide whatever was unworthy to be noticed and give effect to every beautiful and noble attribute." [116] The lamp is the archetypal romantic metaphor of mind, and the use of this metaphor by Hawthorne, in addition to his understanding of the imagination as a mirror, suggests the eclectic breadth of knowledge that informs his view of creativity.

For Hawthorne, reason is the power of mind that arranges, analyzes, and selects the symbols of the heart. It is through the strength of reason or intellect that insights are reproduced and realized in the particular medium that the artist chooses. Reason does not lead to deeper insight; rather, by answering man's instinct for *harmonia*, it orders symbols in such a way that they remain close to the collective experience that initiated them. But when reason is directed away from *harmonia,* and used as a substitute for the power of insight that properly belongs to the imagination, it becomes a "cold tendency, between instinct and intellect," which makes one "pry with a speculative interest into people's passions and impulses." In a moment of self-revelation, Miles Coverdale, in *The Blithedale Romance,* says of this misuse of reason that it "appeared to have gone far towards unhumanizing my heart." [117] Hawthorne would draw one strict limitation on reason: that it can properly be used only to compel the work of art into an arrangement that witnesses to the author's insight. In a sense, this is the most difficult part of the creative process. There are pitfalls on both sides, and Hawthorne is deeply aware of them: either the symbol may be tampered with to the extent that it no longer carries its original meaning, or it may be presented unconvincingly as a vague, formless intuition. This problem stands behind Hawthorne's comment on the scarlet letter that "there was some deep meaning in it, most worthy of interpretation, and which, as it were, streamed forth from the mystic symbol, subtly communicating itself to my sensibilities, but evading the analysis of my mind." [118] Yet Hawthorne recognizes that analysis, the conscious use of language as witness to the symbols of the heart, and hence the handmaiden of expression, is necessary to complete the creative process.

Ultimately, then, Hawthorne believes that the most successful art rises out of a proper relationship between imagination and reason. If this balance fails, and reason is substituted for human sympathies, then, as Melville wrote in his analysis of "Ethan Brand," "the cultivation of the brain eats out the heart." [119] Ethan Brand, in a moment of agony, accuses himself of "the sin of an intellect that triumphed over the sense of brotherhood with man and reverence for God, and sacrificed everything to its own mighty claims! The only sin that deserves a recompense of immortal agony!" [120] It is a fundamental tenet of Hawthorne that if men were to rely only on the intellect "they would be continually changing, so that one age would be entirely unlike another. The great conservative is the heart." [121]

3

A crucial issue that stands behind Hawthorne's comments on the creative process is the problem of how an artist is to know that his insights are valid. Reason cannot validate the imagination; its primary function is to realize "heart-knowledge" in the work of art. Furthermore, in his search for an answer, Hawthorne seems to reject Wordsworth's solution: that the deep truths of nature are also deep in man, and that in moments of imaginative seeing into nature the artist breaks through to the inner truth. Hawthorne never deals specifically with this problem, but a solution is always implied in his treatment of the imagination.

The creative process is its own validation. If an artist is able to work with deep conviction and a feeling of sympathetic response to the problems of man, his insights are automatically validated. In other words, an artist is able to depend on "a certain glow of mind . . . as the sure prognostic of success." [122] The state of mind in which the imagination is fired up, so to speak, furnishes Hawthorne the assurance that his productions are rooted deeply in man's "common nature." Conversely, blocks in the creative process suggest that the artist has been unable to make his personal experience relevant to the totality of man's confrontation with the world. The validation of imaginative insight in the heart is Hawthorne's personal response to the demands of artistic sincerity.

Art, then, is not merely a "slight fancy work," but a creation in which "some sad and awful truths are interwoven." Man — and this is crucial for the artist — "must not disclaim his brotherhood, even with the guiltiest, since, though his hand be clean, his heart has surely been polluted by the flitting phantoms of iniquity. He must feel that, when he shall knock at the gate of heaven, no semblance of an unspotted life can entitle him to entrance there. Penitence must kneel, and Mercy come from the footstool of the throne, or that golden gate will never open!" [123] To an extent, then, Hawthorne would feel that assertions either of man's total depravity, or, on the other hand, of his innate goodness, miss the mark. The cloth of life is woven with good and ill. Sin and guilt, as well as happiness, are necessary, inevitable, and universal. Symbols, created in the heart, reflect this full view of life. A free flowing of the creative process necessarily becomes an affirmation of life in its totality. Hawthorne would agree with Keats as to the nature of the poetical character: "It enjoys light and shade; it lives in gusto, be it foul or fair, high or low, rich or poor, mean or elevated." [124] And he would easily consent to Keats's remark: "Not merely is the heart a horn book, it is the mind's Bible, it is the mind's experience, it is the teat from which the mind or intelligence sucks its identity." [125] The true artist faces the complete range of human experience, and, by the sympathies of his own heart, probes beneath the exterior. "It is his gift — his proudest, but often a melancholy one — to see the inmost soul, and by a power indefinable even to himself, to make it glow or darken upon the canvas, in glances that express the thought and sentiment of years." [126]

Sin in the artist makes him more aware of sin and guilt in others, and hence opens and expands his view of life. So Hester believes that the scarlet letter gives her "a sympathetic knowledge of the sin hidden in other hearts." [127] Or in a notebook entry Hawthorne comments on a diseased infant in the West Derby Workhouse: "This wretched infant had been begotten by Sin upon Disease — diseased Sin was its father, and sinful Disease its mother . . . I can by no means tell how horrible this baby was; neither ought I. And yet its pain and misery seemed to have given it a sort of intelligence; and its eyes stared at me out of their sunken sockets, knowingly, and appealingly." [128] And, similarly, it is Dimmesdale's anguished awareness of his own sin that permits him to deliver a powerful and moving Election Sermon.

The idealists, the reformers, the artists of the fancy, those who would attempt to escape the misery and sin of the world, deny the complex fullness of life. They deny the heart, that "little yet boundless sphere wherein existed the original wrong of which the crime and misery of this outward world were merely types." And unless the reformers hit upon "some method of purifying that foul cavern, forth from it will reissue all the shapes of wrong and misery." "Purify that inward sphere," says Hawthorne, "and the many shapes of evil that haunt the outward, and which now seem almost our only realities, will turn to shadowy phantoms and vanish of their own accord." [129] The point is not that man can abolish evil, nor even, as F. O. Matthiessen claims, that the act of regeneration involves the whole man.[130] Misery and sin are inherent in humanity. To ignore them leads, at best, to a very one-sided vision, and at worst, to a rejection of life. The artist must never attempt to cast the heart into a purifying flame. It is his task to accept both good and evil as they unfold in the course of life. Only in this way does he affirm himself as a man.

Hawthorne's allegory of the heart as cavern comes closest to expressing his sense of the creative character:

At the entrance there is sunshine, and flowers growing about it. You step within, but a short distance, and begin to find yourself surrounded with a terrible gloom, and monsters of divers kinds; it seems like Hell itself. You are bewildered, and wander long without hope. At last a light strikes upon you. You peep towards it, and find yourself in a region that seems in some sort, to reproduce the flowers and sunny beauty of the entrance, but all perfect. These are the depths of the heart, or of human nature, bright and peaceful; the gloom and terror may lie deep; but deeper still is the eternal beauty.[131]

The growth of an artist's perception is, among other things, the subject of this allegory. Life is initially seen only in terms of its surface veneer of happiness. A more mature and deeper vision reveals misery and sin. But in the calm center, where good and evil are blended in a unified impression of life, the artist reaches his most penetrating understanding.

BIBLIOGRAPHY

NOTES

BIBLIOGRAPHY

Abrams, M. H. *The Mirror and the Lamp.* New York, 1958.

Bate, Walter Jackson, ed. *Criticism: the Major Texts.* New York, 1952.

Bell, Millicent. *Hawthorne's View of the Artist.* New York, 1962.

Bernbaum, Ernest, ed. *Anthology of Romanticism.* New York, 1948.

Brownell, W. C. *American Prose Masters.* Cambridge, Mass., 1963.

Charney, Maurice. "Hawthorne and the Gothic Style," *New England Quarterly,* March 1961, pp. 36–49.

Donohue, Agnes M., ed. *A Casebook on the Hawthorne Question.* New York, 1963.

Feidelson, Charles. *Symbolism and American Literature.* Chicago, 1962.

Hart, Walter Morris. "Hawthorne and the Short Story." University of California Press, Berkeley, 1900.

Hawthorne, Julian. *Nathaniel Hawthorne and His Wife,* 2 vols. Cambridge, 1884.

Hawthorne, Nathaniel. *The Complete Works,* ed. George Parsons Lathrop, 12 vols. Cambridge, 1883.

——— *The American Notebooks,* ed. Randall Stewart. New Haven, 1932.

45

———— *The English Notebooks,* ed. Randall Stewart. New York, 1941.

Hoeltje, Hubert H. *Inward Sky: the Mind and Heart of Nathaniel Hawthorne.* Durham, North Carolina, 1962.

Kariel, Henry S. "Man Limited: Nathaniel Hawthorne's Classicism," *South Atlantic Quarterly,* October 1953, pp. 528–542.

Kesselring, Marion L. *Hawthorne's Reading: 1828–1850: A Transcription and Identification of Titles Recorded in the Charge-Books of the Salem Athenaeum.* New York, 1949.

Levin, Harry. *The Power of Blackness.* New York, 1960.

Lewis, R. W. B. *The American Adam: Innocence, Tragedy, and Tradition in the Nineteenth Century.* Chicago, 1955.

Male, Roy R. " 'From the Innermost Germ!' The Organic Principle in Hawthorne's Fiction," *Journal of English Literary History,* 20:218–236 (September,1953).

———— *Hawthorne's Tragic Vision.* Austin, Texas, 1957.

Matthiessen, F. O. *American Renaissance: Art and Expression in the Age of Emerson and Whitman.* New York, 1941.

Perkins, David. *Wordsworth and the Poetry of Sincerity.* Cambridge, Mass., 1964.

Stewart, Randall. *Nathaniel Hawthorne: A Biography.* New Haven, 1948.

Waggoner, Hyatt H. *Hawthorne: A Critical Study.* Cambridge, Mass., 1955.

NOTES

1. Nathaniel Hawthorne, *Passages from the French and Italian Notebooks, The Complete Works of Nathaniel Hawthorne,* ed. George Parsons Lathrop, 12 vols., (Cambridge, Mass., 1883) — hereafter cited as *Works* — X, 98.

2. See Marion L. Kesselring, *Hawthorne's Reading: 1828–1850* (New York, 1949).

3. Nathaniel Hawthorne, as quoted by F. O. Matthiessen, *American Renaissance* (New York, 1941), p. 263.

4. For an evaluation of the loss of innocence as Hawthorne's primary focus see R. W. B. Lewis, *The American Adam* (Chicago, 1955).

5. See Roy R. Male, "The Organic-Mechanical Antithesis," *Hawthorne's Tragic Vision* (Austin, Texas, 1957), pp. 20–37.

6. See M. H. Abrams, *The Mirror and the Lamp* (New York, 1958).

7. Hawthorne borrowed *Carlyle's Miscellany* from the Salem Athenaeum on July 3, 1848, and returned it on August 14. See Kesselring, *Hawthorne's Reading,* p. 41.

8. As quoted by Roy R. Male, *Hawthorne's Tragic Vision,* p. 22.

9. "Old Ticonderoga," *Works,* III, 592.

10. *Works,* I, 16.

11. *Ibid.,* II, 16.

12. Nathaniel Hawthorne, *The English Notebooks,* ed. Randall Stewart (New York, 1941) — hereafter cited as *English Notebooks* — p. 352.

13. See Roy R. Male, " 'From the Innermost Germ!' The Organic Principle in Hawthorne's Fiction," *JELH,* 20:218–236 (September 1953).

14. *The French and Italian Notebooks, Works,* X, 440.

15. For my understanding of Coleridge I am indebted to W. J. Bate, *Criticism: The Major Texts* (New York, 1952).

16. *The French and Italian Notebooks, Works,* X, 132.

17. Bate, *Criticism,* p. 361.

18. *The Marble Faun, Works,* VI, 388.

19. *English Notebooks*, p. 149.

20. For much of my treatment of Hawthorne's view of the Gothic style I am indebted to Maurice Charney, "Hawthorne and the Gothic Style," *NEQ*, March 1961, p. 39.

21. *The French and Italian Notebooks, Works*, X, 282.

22. *English Notebooks*, p. 240.

23. *Ibid.*, p. 413.

24. *Works*, IV, 10 (letter from Hawthorne to Fields of May 23, 1851).

25. See Bate, *Criticism*, p. 6.

26. See Julian Hawthorne, *Nathaniel Hawthorne and His Wife*, 2 vols. (Cambridge, Mass., 1884), I, 209.

27. *The French and Italian Notebooks, Works*, X, 87.

28. See Kesselring, *Hawthorne's Reading*, p. 47, for a list of works by Coleridge that Hawthorne borrowed from the Salem Athenaeum.

29. Manuscript letter in the Berg collection of the New York Public Library, as cited by Randall Stewart in his edition of *The English Notebooks*, p. 654.

30. *English Notebooks*, p. 413.

31. *Works*, IV, 10.

32. *A Wonder-Book, Works*, IV, 13, 135, 136.

33. For this distinction I am indebted to Maurice Charney, "Hawthorne and the Gothic Style."

34. *The House of the Seven Gables, Works*, III, 13.

35. Abrams, *The Mirror and the Lamp*, p. 48.

36. *The Blithdale Romance, Works*, V, 321.

37. Maurice Charney, "Hawthorne and the Gothic Style," is guilty on this score.

38. Henry S. Kariel, "Man Limited: Nathaniel Hawthorne's Classicism," *SAQ*, October 1953, pp. 528–542.

39. This is admirably pointed out by Randall Stewart in his edition of *The English Notebooks*.

40. I am indebted to Randall Stewart's preface to *The English Notebooks* for the substance of this paragraph. See *ibid.*, p. xxxvii.

41. Millicent Bell, *Hawthorne's View of the Artist* (New York, 1962), p. 14.

42. W. C. Brownell, *American Prose Masters*, brings this accusation against Hawthorne.

43. As cited by Julian Hawthorne, *Nathaniel Hawthorne and His Wife*, I, 250.

44. Emerson as cited by Walter Morris Hart, "Hawthorne and the Short Story," University of California Press (Berkeley, 1900), p. 14.

45. *The French and Italian Notebooks, Works,* X, 246.

46. Nathaniel Hawthorne, *The American Notebooks,* ed. Randall Stewart (New Haven, 1932) — hereafter cited as *American Notebooks* — p. 189.

47. As cited by Julian Hawthorne, *Nathaniel Hawthorne and His Wife*, I, 261.

48. "Rappaccini's Daughter," *Works,* II, 128.

49. "The Intelligence Office," *Works,* II, 374–375.

50. "The Old Manse," *Works,* II, 44.

51. *Ibid.,* 43.

52. "The Haunted Mind," *Works,* I, 343, 345.

53. *Anthology of Romanticism,* ed. Ernest Bernbaum (New York, 1948), pp. 176–177.

54. *Ibid.,* p. 400.

55. "The Haunted Mind," *Works,* I, 346.

56. As cited by Matthiessen, *American Renaissance,* p. 233.

57. *American Notebooks,* p. 105.

58. "Fire Worship," *Works,* II, 167.

59. "Rappaccini's Daughter," *Works,* II, 125, 128.

60. *The Blithedale Romance, Works,* V, 502.

61. "The Custom House," *Works,* V, 54.

62. *The Scarlet Letter, Works,* V, 155.

63. *American Notebooks,* p. 106.

64. "The Custom House," *Works,* V, 57.

65. Preface to *The Snow-Image, Works,* III, 386.

66. "The Village Uncle," *Works,* I, 356.

67. Preface to *The Snow-Image, Works,* III, 388.

68. This phrase was coined by Wilhelm Worringer in *Abstraktion und Einfühlung* (1908).

69. For these ideas on "abstraction" in art I am indebted to T. E. Hulme, *Speculations: Essays on Humanism and the Philosophy of Art,* (1924).

70. Preface to *Twice-Told Tales, Works,* I, 16.

71. "Drowne's Wooden Image," *Works,* II, 352.

49

72. *Works*, II, 481.

73. *The French and Italian Notebooks, Works*, X, 336.

74. *Ibid.*, p. 124. For these examples I am indebted to Millicent Bell, *Hawthorne's View of the Artist*.

75. *The Marble Faun, Works*, VI, 25, 161, 162–163, 25.

76. *Twice-Told Tales, Works*, I, 17.

77. Kesselring, *Hawthorne's Reading*, p. 39.

78. Coleridge, as quoted by Bate in *Criticism*, p. 387.

79. See Bate, *Criticism*, p. 324.

80. *English Notebooks*, p. 240.

81. "The Custom House," *Works*, V, 56.

82. *The House of the Seven Gables, Works*, III, 199, 200.

83. *The Marble Faun, Works*, VI, 63.

84. "P.'s Corespondence," *Works*, II, 420.

85. *Ibid.*, p. 412.

86. "Drowne's Wooden Image," *Works*, II, 350, 354, 355, 362, 362.

87. Letter to Sophia; see Julian Hawthorne, *Hawthorne and His Wife*, I, 209.

88. "The Artist of the Beautiful," *Works*, II, 507, 535–536.

89. "The Old Manse," *Works*, II, 24.

90. *American Notebooks*, p. 122.

91. William Wordsworth, *Poetical Works*, ed. Ernest de Selincourt and Helen Darbishire (Oxford, 1949–1958), II, 385.

92. Hawthorne borrowed Coleridge's *Aids to Reflection* from the Salem Athenaeum on July 13, 1883. See Kesselring.

93. Coleridge, *Aids to Reflection*, as quoted by David Perkins, *Wordsworth and the Poetry of Sincerity* (Cambridge, Mass., 1964), p. 87.

94. This is a paraphrase of David Perkins, p. 276, n. 5.

95. As quoted by Bate in *Criticism*, p. 386.

96. "The Custom House," *Works*, V, 55.

97. *The French and Italian Notebooks, Works*, X, 162–163.

98. Hawthorne attributes this ability to Pearl, *The Scarlet Letter*, *Works*, V, 120.

99. *The Scarlet Letter, Works*, V, 210.

100. The suggestion is made by David Perkins.

101. *American Notebooks*, p. 107.

102. "The Old Manse," *Works*, II, 31.

103. *The Marble Faun, Works*, VI, 388.
104. *The House of the Seven Gables, Works*, III, 59.
105. "The Old Manse," *Works*, II, 16.
106. *The House of the Seven Gables, Works*, III, 332.
107. "The Old Manse," *Works*, II, 32.
108. See Matthiessen, *American Renaissance*, p. 259.
109. "Feathertop: A Moralized Legend," *Works*, II, 276, 276.
110. See Matthiessen, *American Renaissance*, p. 264.
111. As quoted by Matthiessen, *American Renaissance*, p. 264.
112. "Monsieur du Miroir," *Works*, II, 191, 194.
113. *The Scarlet Letter, Works*, V, 176, 207.
114. *The House of the Seven Gables, Works*, III, 377.
115. "The Haunted Mind," *Works*, I, 346.
116. "A Select Party," *Works*, II, 71.
117. *The Blithedale Romance, Works*, V, 495.
118. "The Custom House," *Works*, V, 50.
119. As quoted by Matthiessen, *American Renaissance*, p. 345.
120. *Ibid.*, p. 346.
121. *Ibid.*, p. 347.
122. "Passages from a Relinquished Work," *Works*, II, 471.
123. "Fancy's Show Box," *Works*, I, 257.
124. Bernbaum, *Anthology of Romanticism*, p. 845.
125. *Ibid.*, p. 850.
126. "The Prophetic Pictures," *Works*, I, 202.
127. *The Scarlet Letter, Works*, V, 89.
128. *English Notebooks*, p. 276.
129. "Earth's Holocaust," *Works*, II, 455.
130. Matthiessen, *American Renaissance*, p. 347.
131. *American Notebooks*, p. 98.